TELL ME
ABOUT
WRITERS

ENID BLYTON

Acknowledgements

For permission to reproduce copyright material, the author and publishers gratefully acknowledge the following:

Gillian Baverstock, cover, back cover, 5 (left), 6, 7 (top), 8, 9 (bottom), 10 (bottom), 11(top), 12, 13 (bottom), 14, 16 (top), 17 (right), 19, 20, 21;
Enid Blyton Limited, title page, 5 (right), 10 (top), 15, 16 (bottom two), 17 (left), 18;
Bromley Libraries, 7 (bottom);
St Christopher's The Hall School, Beckenham, 9 (top);
Great Ormond Street Hospital, 11 (bottom);
Mr and Mrs D. P. Hawthorne, 13 (top).

Enid Blyton's signature mark is a trademark of Enid Blyton Limited.

For further information on Enid Blyton please contact WWW.blyton.com

TELL ME ABOUT WRITERS

ENID BLYTON

written by
Gillian Baverstock

Evans

Evans Brothers Limited

Published by Evans Brothers Limited
2A Portman Mansions
Chiltern Street
London W1U 6NR

First published 1997
Reprinted 1998, 2001
First published in paperback by
Evans Brothers Limited in 2004

Printed in China by WKT Company Ltd

British Library Cataloguing in Publication data.

Baverstock, Gillian
  Tell me about Enid Blyton
  1. Blyton, Enid, 1898?-1968 – Juvenile literature 2. Women
  novelists, English – 20th century – Biography – Juvenile
  literature
  I. Title II. Enid Blyton
  823.9'12

ISBN 0237526190

Enid Blyton wrote more than 700 books for children. Enid was my mother. Let me tell you about her.

Enid was born in London in 1897, more than a hundred years ago. Her parents Thomas and Theresa had just moved from Sheffield. Thomas loved baby Enid very much. Once, he held her in his arms all night when she nearly died of whooping cough. In the morning she was much better.

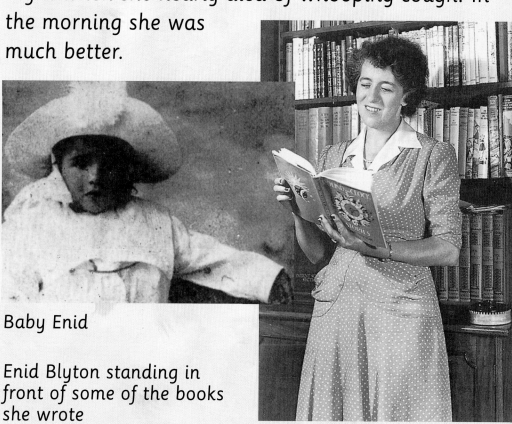

Baby Enid

Enid Blyton standing in front of some of the books she wrote

The Blyton family soon moved to Beckenham in Kent. Here, Enid's two brothers, Hanly and Carey were born. Enid hated looking after her little brothers and helping her mother in the house. She spent all the time she could with her father.

Enid aged seven

The house in Beckenham where the Blyton family lived

Enid's father
Thomas

They worked in the garden together and went for long walks in the woods and fields. Enid loved to read and her father gave her lots of books. A favourite book was "Alice in Wonderland" by Lewis Carroll. When she was older, she read all her father's books, even his encyclopedias.

Beckenham looked like this when Enid Blyton lived there.

Enid Blyton = Enid Blyton = Enid Blyton =

Enid's father left home when she was thirteen. He had been her best friend and she missed him very much. Now she was only really happy at school. Sometimes she got into trouble for playing tricks in class. She and her friends had fun writing to each other in code.

A letter in code from Enid to a friend

Enid played lacrosse at school. She was very good at games and English but she hated maths.

little mademoiselle sends for her love. annecy 30th July

St Christopher's School in Beckenham, where Enid was a pupil

The book of poems that Enid's mother gave her

Enid liked writing. She wrote little plays and songs for school concerts. When she was fourteen she won a poetry competition. She wrote stories and sent them to magazines, but no one wanted to print them. Her mother was cross because she thought Enid was wasting her time, but she did give Enid a book of poems for her sixteenth birthday.

When Enid was nineteen, she left home to train as a teacher. She loved teaching, and in the holidays she could write her stories. In 1992 her first book was published. It was a book of poems called "Child Whispers". An old schoolfriend drew the picture for the cover.

The cover of Enid Blyton's first book

Enid Blyton with her first pupils

Two years later, Enid married a publisher called Hugh Pollock. Enid stopped teaching and worked for a teachers' magazine. The teachers read her stories to their classes and lots of children wrote to her. Often there were so many letters she could not answer them all. So she put money in her collecting box for Great Ormond Street Hospital instead.

Enid and Hugh on their wedding day

She also wrote a little magazine called "Sunny Stories". She was so busy she had to learn to type.

GETTING WELL
THANK YOU
THE HOSPITAL FOR SICK CHILDREN.
GREAT ORMOND ST. LONDON, W.C.I.

Enid had a collecting box like this one

11

THE LONDON BOROUGH OF BROMLEY
ENID BLYTON
1897 – 1968
AUTHORESS
lived here

This plaque is now on the front of Elfin Cottage (right)

Enid Blyton loved gardening.

Enid and Hugh lived in a house called Elfin Cottage. They turned a field into a beautiful garden. Afterwards she wrote a book called "Let's garden". When I was little I was cross because my mother would not let me build a pond, although her book told me exactly how to do it!

12

Old Thatch
today

In 1929 Enid and Hugh moved
to Old Thatch. This is where I
was born. My sister Imogen
was born four years later.
In the evenings, when
nanny took baby Imogen
for her bath, Enid read
me the stories she had
written that day. She
even made up stories
about my doll, Amelia Jane,
who was very naughty!

Amelia Jane

13

I loved being with my mother. We often walked down the lane and along the river with the dogs.

When Enid was little she was not allowed to have pets. Once she found a lost kitten, but her mother gave it away. So now she had lots of pets - two terriers, three Siamese cats, pigeons, doves, a tortoise, goldfish and some hens!

One of Enid's dogs

Enid gives me a hug because I am frightened of the lambs!

Enid Blyton at work at Green Hedges

One of the books Enid wrote at Green Hedges

In 1938 we moved to a bigger house, called Green Hedges. Enid Blyton wrote all her well-known books here.

My favourite book was "Secret Island". In it, the children build a house of willow branches which start to grow. I planted a willow twig to see if it would really grow. It did - into an enormous tree!

The Second World War began in 1939. During the war Enid's first marriage ended, and she married a doctor. We all went on holidays together to the seaside in Dorset. After one holiday there, she wrote the first Famous Five book, "Five on a Treasure Island".

In wartime, paper for printing books was very hard to get. "Mary Mouse" was printed on paper strips left over from another book.

Enid's daughters, Gillian and Imogen

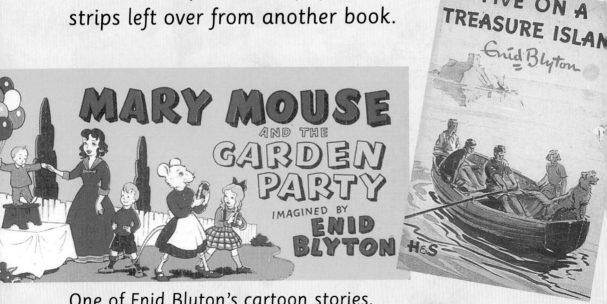

One of Enid Blyton's cartoon stories, printed on leftover paper

After the war Enid met a Dutch artist called Harmsen Van Der Beek. He painted brightly coloured little people. Enid loved his pictures. She asked him to paint the pictures for her next book. That week, Enid wrote the first two Noddy books.

A model of Noddy

Noddy and Big Ears, painted by Van Der Beek

Enid became busier than ever. In the next ten years she wrote two hundred books, a Noddy pantomime, two Famous Five films and a play.

She ran four clubs through the new "Enid Blyton's Magazine". Children who joined the clubs collected money to help children in need.

Children from all over the world wrote to her. She read every letter and tried to answer each one.

A scene from a new Famous Five television programme

Enid Blyton could write a book in a week. She sat down with her typewriter and closed her eyes. After a few minutes, children came into her mind, laughing and talking. She saw the places where everything would happen. Then the story filled her mind and she wrote it down as fast as she could.

Enid and her husband Kenneth look at a new story

Enid Blyton checks her latest book at the printers.

19

Enid kept on writing until she became ill. She died in 1968, when she was seventy-one years old. She always loved talking to children and telling them stories. Today children still love to read her stories, and watch films of her books.

Children from all over the world wrote to their favourite author, Enid Blyton.

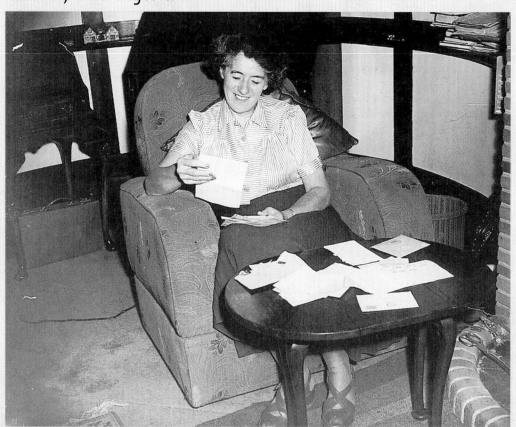

Important dates

1897 Enid Blyton was born

1907 She went to St. Christopher's School for Girls in Beckenham

1910 Her father left home

1916 Started at teacher training college

1919 First teaching job in Bickley, Kent

1922 Her first book "Child Whispers" was published

1924 Married Hugh Pollock

1926 Moved to Elfin Cottage

1929 Moved to Old Thatch

1931 First daughter Gillian born

1935 Second daughter Imogen born

1938 Moved to Green Hedges; "The Secret Island" published

1942 First Famous Five novel published; divorced Hugh Pollock

1943 Married Kenneth Darrell Waters

1949 Met artist Van Der Beek; "Little Noddy Goes to Toyland" published; First Secret Seven book published

1967 Kenneth Darrell Waters died

1968 Enid Blyton died

Enid Blyton's favourite garden statue. A silver model of it called the Enid Blyton Award is to be given each year to someone who has helped children.

Keywords

artist
someone who makes
drawings and paintings

encyclopedia
a book or series of books
with information on many
subjects, arranged in
alphabetical order

magazine
like a book with pictures,
which is published regularly

publisher
someone who produces
books or magazines for sale

Index